On A Schoolmaster.

Here lie Willie Michie's banes;
O Satan, when ye tak him,
Gi'e him the schoolin' o' your weans,
For clever de'ils he'll mak 'em!

ROBERT BURNS

ALLAN MORRISON

'Oor Wee School
Wis A Rare Wee School!'

ILLUSTRATED BY

www.vitalspark.co.uk

The Vital Spark is an imprint of
Neil Wilson Publishing
www.nwp.co.uk

© Allan Morrison, 2013
First published in 2000
Reprinted 2001, 2002, 2005, 2007, 2013

The author has established his moral right to be
identified as the author of this work.

All illustrations © Rupert Besley, 2013

A catalogue record for this book is available
from the British Library.

ISBN: 978-1-903238-14-1
Ebook ISBN: 978-1-906476-81-6

Typeset in Bodoni
Designed by Mark Blackadder

Printed and bound in Poland

Contents

Preface

Do you remember…

…your first day at school? Half the weans were in tears – the other half were greetin'.

The revolving blackboard invented by Kilsyth joiner Wullie Garden that meant the teacher could stuff twice as much in yer heid at the wan time.

The dreadful punishments – "Go and sit with the girls." Equal to at least six of the best – with your hands crossed!

Lining up in the playground each day, and clumpin' proudly into school to the sounds of a piano being demolished.

Walkin' tae the school tae save yer pennies. Then you could buy cinnamon sticks and single Woodbine, to smoke in the school's cludgie.

The books in which you practiced writing; up thin and doon thick.

Ink wells that contained more refuse and junk than the average midden.

Usin' a wooden rule tae flick bits o' blottin' paper, soddin' wi' ink, across the class.

In the playground playing 'skitey' wi' cigarette cards, and 'pappie' using the tops off milk bottles. Your mother making you a wee bag to hold your bools (marbles). There were steelies, plunkers, brown dawds and glassies – and you could play Moshie with them. Or if you had lost all your bools you might play 'Ali Bali, Ali Bali, who's got the ball?'

Waiting outside the headmaster's room. The same feeling as you must get on 'Death Row'.

Sittin' still wi' yer arms folded – so that you

could be the milk monitor that day and maybe get an extra wee bottle!

Peever beds at playtime on a hot summer's day … sheer magic!

The Dominie, the Heidie, who was clad in a frock coat, spats and a tile hat. Him and God were wan an' the same.

Being desperate to get to school to use the toilets … as the cludgie on your landin' was always occupied in the morning.

Being 'het' at hiding-seek or tig. You had to go and find the others or stay in the 'den' in the school shed. Some folk were forever shouting, 'Keys'!, or, 'The game's a bogie!'

Shoutin' at someone in the playground …
'Tell-tale tit, .
Your mammy cannae knit,
Your daddy cannae go to bed
without his dummy tit!'

Tell-tale tit,
Your tongue will be slit
And all the dogs in Scotland
Will get a little bit.

THE CLIPE

Being instructed by the Headie
at assembly, that in the case of an
air-raid you must go to the nearest
shelter –'And don't forget your
red and white Mickey Mouse
gas masks!'

Skippin' in the playground to
the likes of …

'A hunner and ninety-nine,
Ma faither got in a byne
Ma mither came oot wi' the
     washin' cloot
And skelped his big, fat behind.'

or

'Hey, Jock ma cuddy,
ma cuddy's o'er the dyke,
and if you touch ma cuddy
ma cuddy'll gie ye a bite.'

or

'Kirn, Dunoon, Innellan, Rothesay,
Kirn, Dunoon, Innellan, Rothesay … '
(ad infinitum!)

or

'Heybab-a ree bab,
Ma mammy's got a prefab!'

The day all the children got their very special
Victory Celebration letter from King George the
Sixth – "We wan the war!"

The massive game of football in the playground,
umpteen-a-side. You had to find someone who

wanted to join in at the same time. And then it was 'cock' or 'hen' to determine which team you joined. Some weans even got a kick o' the ba'!

The jannie who always seemed to be in his wee howff in the school dunny; or if not, could be heard shoutin' at the weans, "Come here, you, or I'll kick yer bahoochie!"

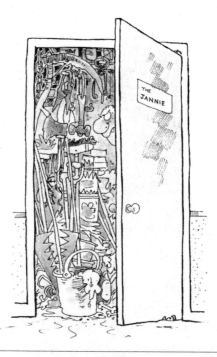

THE JANNIE

The rhythmic chantin' in unison of multiplication tables for half-an-hour every day, so that nowadays, when someone asks you, for example, "Whit's nine times twelve?" you don't even have tae think o' the answer. It's engraved inside yer heid – and oot it just comes ... A hunner and eight!

In winter goin' doon an icy slide in the playground – wan leg afore the ither.

Havin' to walk to school – unless you were lucky and had a gird wi' a cleet!

The first few classes at school – where you didn't get the strap if you were bad – you just got a palmie.

The playground divided in two by sex. No girl or boy would have been seen dead in the other half.

Winding stairs that took you up to an echoing corridor – and the all pervading smell of weans from the last hunner years.

The smell of steaming, wet trench coats hung in the cloakrooms on a rainy morning.

Pupils sitting in pairs at double-width desks, which had a single lid over a large compartment, holding text books and jotters. Individual lift-up seats, in plain wood in an iron frame.

… Those were the days!

Introduction

Oor wee school's a rerr wee school,
It's made wi' bricks an plaster,
But the only thing that's wrang wi' it
Is the baldy heided master.

He goes to the pub on Saturday,
He goes to the church on Sunday
To pray to the Lord tae gae him strength,
Tae belt the weans on Monday!

So goes the old Scots song much loved by generations of schoolchildren, though nowadays, with the abolition of the belt, the last line has been changed to 'shout at the weans on Monday!' Whether you liked school or loathed it, there was no escaping education in Scotland. School made a significant impression on us all. In fact most folks can remember quite a few of the teachers from both their Primary and Secondary schools. Some can even recite most classmates' names, even without the class photograph.

Every school was unique. It had its own atmosphere, its own smells (many from the children!) and its own culture. The teachers, formidable, perjinkety, stern or kindly, together with their nicknames, live on with us. Many had that special requirement of all good teachers – the knack of making any subject interesting. And who could forget the jannie ringing the school bell.

We all have vivid memories – even scars from our schooldays. We were shaped by men and women who taught us in their own distinctive ways; sometimes with caustic wit and rapier-sharp tongues.

And do you remember the 'Holy of Holies' – the Headie's room? If you found yourself there before the early eighties, then it could only be for one thing. And it was sore! The problem was that if you went home and told your parents you got another one!

So, what did we learn from our teachers? Wisdom, that if applied universally would make the world a better place; play hard but fair, be tolerant of others, and continue to educate yourself right throughout life. And of course the three 'R's ... hammered into us until we could all contest *Mastermind* in parsing, grammar, comprehension and mental arithmetic.

Whether your education took place in a wood-panelled school with tiled corridors, in the Borders, or in a one-classroomed building set in the Highlands, we can all remember some humorous event from school which stays in the memory bank, and when we recall it now and again, it makes us chuckle.

Oor Wee School Wis A Rare Wee School! is a collection of such tales from around Scotland. They

come from an educational system of world renown
where we all spent interesting and purposeful years.
I am deeply indebted to those people who, mostly
with a smile and sparkling eyes, have kindly passed
them on to me for this publication. Strictly on the
basis of anonymity, of course!

Allan Morrison

1. Days Long Gone at the Schule

The schoolchildren at a Clydeside school, had all recently returned from a period of evacuation in Rothesay. They were clearly unsettled by reports of German bombings of various towns and cities.

"Miss, will they bomb this school while we're in it?" asked one wee, apprehensive pupil.

"Certainly not!" came the wise response. "Hitler's Granny lives up the close in the tenement next to this school."

All the children were much relieved, but thereafter glanced apprehensively into that particular close whenever they passed.

From a class first-aid exam some fifty-odd years ago.
Q. If you found your teacher on the floor and there was a smell of gas, what would you do?
A. Put a shilling in the meter and run!

*   *   *

"Murray, what is the meaning of the word, 'posh'?" asked the teacher in a school on the south side of Glasgow.

"Havin' a cludgie on the landin' a' tae yersel', miss, wi' a real chain instead o' string hangin' frae the cistern."

*   *   *

The one class-roomed Highland school served a community south of Oban. One day it was visited by an H.M. Inspector. Taking the register from the teacher, he quickly stabbed at a name.

"MacDougall. Stand up!" He ordered. Half the class stood.

"Right, sit down!" he bellowed. His finger found another name.

"Campbell. Stand up!"

This time the other half of the class stood up.

*   *   *

It was the first day of school for the children of primary one, at a small school in Irvine, in 1936. To settle the excited children down, the young teacher gave each of her new charges a ball of plasticine to play with.

Once the children were engrossed in making snakes, little men and women etc, the teacher counted her pupils. Then she counted them again, as she had one too many; thirty-two instead of thirty-one. So she went round each child, ticking off names, until she came to one small boy whose name was not on the register.

"You're not on my list, McGillicuddy." The wee chap looked blank. "Who did you come to school with this morning?" she demanded.

"Ma cousins fae the farm, miss."

"And what age are you, McGillicuddy?"

"Four, miss."

"Four! You're too young. You've got to be five to be here. Away back to the farm for another year."

"But, miss, noo I'll only hae the coos tae play wi'!"

*　　　*　　　*

The report cards were given out to the class to take home to have their parents sign. One boy opened the envelope and was somewhat dismayed at the contents.

Staying behind at the end of the day, he asked with an engaging smile. " Could you not add something good, miss?"

"And what could I possibly add that would be

3

good?" queried the teacher.

"How about, 'Always brings his gas mask to school'?"

* * *

"Where is James McDuff today?" demanded 'Black Aggie', the formidable teacher of a war-time class in Glasgow.

Please, miss, he sprained his ankle last night, playin' wi' an old bomb doon in the bombed buildings."

"Huh – that's a dud excuse!"

* * *

In the darkest days of 1942, a Paisley teacher suspected she was being somewhat patronised by one of the pupils.

"Simpson, I think you're just buttering me up."

"What's butter, miss?" came the innocent response.

* * *

A boy in 1941 brought a banana to a Glasgow school. None of the pupils had ever tasted banana. The teacher carefully cut it up into forty-four slices for everyone to try.

* * *

To teach the children the lesson of "doing a job well", the pupils at Ardnamurchan primary school were required to bring a piece of peat to school each morning. If the peat was broken the offender got the strap!

*   *   *

A boy entered a Glasgow classroom and asked the teacher, if his own teacher, Mr McLean, could borrow his Lochgelly (strap).

At lunchtime it transpired that the boy was leaving school that day, and he had gone around each teacher with the same request. That put the kybosh on beltings at the school, until replacements arrived some days later.

*　　*　　*

"What is the purpose of a barrage-balloon, McPherson?" demanded the teacher of an Airdrie school, in 1939.

As no answer was forthcoming, the teacher posed a slightly different question. "Where do balloons go, McPherson?"

"To the top of the class, sir."

"Come out here and hold out your hand!"

*　　*　　*

"Watson, you smell of soot," sniffed the teacher at a Glasgow school to a ricketty, wee pupil.

"Yes, miss. Last night ma mammy set the' chimney oan fire, tae save havin' tae get the sweep."

*　　*　　*

The Paisley teacher could see Jimmy was scratching away furiously.

"Why are you scratching yourself?" she demanded.

"Because 'am the only wan that knows where I'm itchy, miss."

*　　*　　*

"Simpson, what would you like to work as?"

"A doctor, sir."

"Excellent – and you, Agnew?"

"A policemen, sir."

"Very good. Now you MacDuff, what would you like to do – though I'm almost frightened to ask?"

"A'd like to be a back-green singer. Aw ye dae is learn wan song and wummen throw doon money at ye."

*   *   *

The children in the class were all grinning, some tittering.

"What's the big joke this morning!" demanded the teacher.

"It's McCulloch's flat skippit bunnet," ventured one brave wee soul.

"McCulloch, let's all see this famous bunnet!"

"Sir, it wis rainin' sore this morn, and ma mither told me to wear ma faither's old doo-lander. As a wis comin' in the school gate – a seagull shitted on it."

*   *   *

The children at a Hamilton school were all in the drill (gym) hall going through a variety of exercises to the instructions of a voice from a BBC Scotland schools' radio programme.

The sound suddenly stopped. So did the children.

They looked around somewhat confused at each other, when a different voice from the wireless announced.

"King George the sixth has died."

All the children silently filed out, and were sent home early.

*   *   *

"Sharp! Why are you late?" demanded the teacher in a Glasgow school.

"Sorry, sir, but ma mammy says she's at death's door, and ma daddy's away tae get the doctor tae try to pull her through."

*   *   *

"And what would you like to do as a career, Barry?" asked a teacher in an educational establishment in Irvine.

"Well, sir, I've half a mind to go into teaching."

"That's all you'll need, Barry!"

*   *   *

"You're late, Howard!"

"Sorry, sir. I upset an old biddy up oor wally close this morning. When I walked doon the stairs she'd just pipe-clayed them."

"So, what happened, Howard?"

"She made me pipe-clay them again, and pit doon newspaper on each stair."

"Sit down, Howard. You've suffered enough this morning."

*　　　*　　　*

"Sir, I've goat a job," informed one enthusiastic lad at a school in Clydebank.

"I never thought anybody would give a right comedian like you a job, McNeish."

"It's on a soor-dook cart"

"Aye, well, if you drink that stuff it'll take the glaikit smile off your face."

*　　　*　　　*

It was the Friday test at a Dundee school. This week it was geography. The children were all keen to do well, because it determined who got gold stars, silver stars or bronze stars; also who had to clean the blackboard during the forthcoming week.

"Please, miss, I'm gonnae do well in the geography test," announced George.

"My, somebody's got a great conceit of themselves," replied the teacher. " Just remember, George, to keep a cool head. And this time don't put down Ben Nevis as a boy's name!"

*   *   *

Every morning at playtime, wee Joe's mother came to the school railings, and passed him in his play-piece in a poke. Some days it was just a piece with sugar on it, but if he was very good, and his father had brought home most of his wages the previous Friday, he got a chocolate biscuit.

Joe was one of the most popular boys in the school – well, certainly during the five minutes after his mother passed the wee poke through to him.

*   *   *

It was the 11th of November, 1918. The Greenock class were told that the Great War was over and armistice declared. Fathers and brothers would be coming home.

They observed a two-minute silence, and listened to the Headmaster give a short account of the war, before singing *God Save the King*. When the Headmaster left the classroom, everyone stood on the top of the desks hollering and shouting. The teacher climbed on a table and joined in the celebrations. Another teacher quietly played the piano in the hall and wept; her fiancée had been killed the previous year.

*   *   *

A mother in the twenties wrote the following note to her son's teacher.

'Excuse David being absent two days as he was at Hamilton being birched. I have the honour to be, His Mother.'

*   *   *

One of the young boys at a Crieff school in the twenties was given a handsome watch. Unfortunately he could not tell the time by looking at it. This led to some fun in the playground.

"What's the time, Arnold?"

Arnold would think for a minute and then produce the famous watch. He would hold it up so everyone could see it and say, "Wid ye believe it. It's that time already."

*   *   *

It was Rab's turn to put coal on the classroom fire in an Edinburgh school, but he tended to be a lazy boy. One morning, Old Corky, the teacher shouted from

his desk. "Quick, boys and girls – fire!"
The pupils were all concerned. "Where's the fire,
sir?"

Giving Rab a withering look the teacher replied,
"In every class but ours!"

*　　　*　　　*

He had lived in Canada for many years. Now in his
eighties he remained fit and alert, his blue eyes
twinkling, the Scots accent still intact.

"You could put a blindfold on me and take me
round a' the schools in Scotland and I'd tell you
when it wis ma school. You see, it had it's own special
smell, its own atmosphere, its own sounds. It wis ma
wee school."

*　　　*　　　*

An old Kilmacolm farmer remembered his schooldays thus:

"Few books were used besides the Bible and
Shorter Catechism or 'Questions' as we called the
hated task book. Long stretches of the Bible were
read, finishing off the day with singing Psalm tunes.
Kilmarnock, *Coleshill*, and *Evan* were the
favourites."

*　　　*　　　*

A Dumfriesshire mother visited her child's teacher with the following warning:

"I've just come to tell ye ye'll no' hiv to dunch Maggie in the back. Ye see, Maggie has a gless e'e. The last teacher gied her a dunch, an oot cam' the e'e, an' doon went the teacher in a faint. So ye'll ken to be careful!"

*   *   *

One of the school pupils at an Edinburgh School in the mid 1800s, had the job of putting oil in the classroom lamps during the winter. When gas lamps were introduced he was heard to say:

"I litted them last week and they have never needed fillin' since."

*   *   *

Notice on the door of a Glasgow School.

'The School Board wish to henceforth discourage the use of slates. Where possible, jotters should be made available. This is due to the children's unfortunate habit of spitting on slates before wiping them clean. This carries the possible risk of the spreading of disease.'

*   *   *

In wet weather the children at a Rutherglen school used to crowd into an open shed at the far end of the playground. There they sang at the top of their voices.

"If I had an egg, I'd have ham and egg for breakfast – if only I had some ham!"

*   *   *

In 1914 a War Map was presented to a Renfrewshire school in order that the children could be informed of the progress of the war. The expectation was that the children would be able to follow on the map the advances and eventual victory of the British forces against the Germans. Because of the stalemate at the Front the map was never updated. It hung on the wall until 1919.

*   *   *

It was in the 1930's and the Glasgow School Board had an evening meeting to which all parents and friends had been invited. Towards the end of the evening, the headmistress, an unmarried lady of advancing years commented, "If you wish any advice on your child's education or upbringing, feel free to consult with myself."

This brought a loud response from one mother. "Her advise me! Me who's buried three o' them!"

*   *   *

The Education (Scotland) Act 1872. Compulsory Clause.

'Every parent is obliged to ensure that his or her

children between the ages of 5 and 13 are taught Reading, Writing and Arithmetic.'

(Although Education was not free, poverty was deemed not to be an excuse for keeping children at home. Needy parents could apply to the Parochial Board of the parish for assistance in paying school fees.)

*　　　*　　　*

One elderly lady in Glasgow remembered, "It was during the time of the First World War and the school decided to form a school choir. I certainly didn't want to sing in it, but we all were tested. I did my utmost to sing out of tune, but to my chagrin the beguiling Miss Thompson just said, "You have a lovely voice. You're in."

*　　　*　　　*

In the twenties there was considerable rivalry between the pupils of the Old Burgh School, Chapel Street, Rutherglen, (Headmaster, 'Yuckie' Aitken,) and the Free Church School in Glasgow Road. (Headmaster, Mr Summers). The boy's war cry between the schools ran thus:

"Summers' scholars are a' in a raw,
An ounce of tobacco would ding them a'."
The retort to this was:
"Aitken's scholars are lame as duck,

Send then all quacking to old Yuckie, Yuck yuck!"

*   *   *

The subject was health and the teacher in a Perthshire school had drawn the outline of the human form on the blackboard.

The class made not a bad guess at where the heart was, and the kidneys. But when asked the question, "Where is the colon?" they seemed stuck until one child stuck her hand up.

"Please, miss, the fire."

*   *   *

All pupils in an Edinburgh school who offended by using bad language were sent to the Headmaster. They had their mouths washed out with carbolic soap followed by two of the tawse. Very few re-offended.

Playground Songs and Poems

A Scottish playground is a superb source of information gathering. It is there that many children not only learn the facts of life ... they also got to know the many wonderful songs and rhymes compiled over the generations.

*　　　*　　　*

Kiltie, kiltie cauld bum
Three stairs up;
The wummin in the middle door
Hit me wi' a cup.
The cup wis full o' jelly
It hit me in the belly;
Kiltie, kiltie cauld bum
Three stairs up.

*　　　*　　　*

The boy stood on the burning deck
His feet were full o' blisters;
The fire burned his troosers aff
So he pit oan his sister's.

*　　　*　　　*

Wee, chookie birdie, hoh hoh hoh,
Laid an egg on the window sill
The window sill began tae crack
Wee chookie birdie, quack quack quack.

*　　　*　　　*

No' last night but the night afore
Three, wee witches came to ma door
One had a fiddle, one had a drum
And one had a pancake stuck up her bum.

*   *   *

One, two, three a-leary
Four, five, six a-leary
seven, eight, nine a-leary
ten a-leary postman.

*   *   *

One. two. three, ma mammy caught a flea
She put in the sugar bowl
And had it in her tea.

One, two,three, ma mammy caught a flea,
She roasted it, and toasted it
And had it fur her tea.

One, two three, ma mammy caught a flea,
She put it in the chip pan
And fried it for her tea.

* * *

Paddy on the railway
Picking up stones
Alang came an engine
And broke Paddy's bones
Oh, says Paddy, 'That's no' fair'
Oh, says the engine driver
'Ye shouldnae huv been there.'

* * *

Ye cannae catch me fur a wee bawbee
Ha, ha, ha; he he he.

* * *

There is a happy land.
Doon at Oor Wee School.
There a' the children stand,
An the teachers rule.
Pen and ink ye never see
Dirty water fur yer tea,
It's a life o' misery
Doon at Oor Wee School.

* * *

Sticks and stones may break ma bones
But names will never hurt me
When you're dead and in the grun
You'll be sorry what you called me.

       *   *   *

Sugarally watter
Black as the lum
Shoogle up the bottle
And we'll all get some.

       *   *   *

The bell, the bell, the B-E-L,
Tell the teacher I'm no' well
If yer late, run like hell
The bell, the bell, the B-E-L.

       *   *   *

I'm Shirley Temple
With the curly, curly hair
Dimples in my cheeks
And my clothes are up to there.
I'm not able
To do the Betty Grable
I'm Shirley Temple
With the curly, curly hair.

*   *   *

Who'll come in to ma wee ring?
Ma wee ring, ma wee ring
Who'll come in to ma wee ring?
To mak' it a wee bit bigger.

*   *   *

Dan, Dan the funny wee man
Washed his face in the frying pan
Combed his hair wi' the leg o' the chair,
Dan, Dan the funny wee man.

*   *   *

Eeny meeny miny mo,
Catch a nipper by the toe
If he squeals let him go
Eeny meeny miny mo.

*   *   *

One fine day in the middle o' the night
Two dead men got up to fight
Back to back they faced each other
Drew their swords and shot each other

*   *   *

We're doon in the jungle
Livin' in a tent;
Better than a prefab,
Nae rent!

*   *   *

Rainy, rainy, rattlestanes,
Dinna rain on me;
Rain on John O'Groat's hoose
Faur ower the sea.

*   *   *

Hokie, pokie, penny pie,
Stand ye aw oot by.

*   *   *

One child makes a craw's nest using the first and
second finger of both hands. They then chant,

"Pit yer finger in the craw's nest-
The craw's no' in.

The craw's at the back door
Peckin' at a pin!"

Another child pokes a finger into the craw's nest as the craw's no' in. The child making the 'nest' then nips the other's finger with the left thumb and says, "The craw's at the backdoor peckin' at the pin!"

* * *

"Round and round the rugged rock, the ragged rascal ran. If you can tell me how many 'R's are in that, I'll call you a clever man!"

* * *

"This is the way the teacher stands;
This is the way she holds her hands;
This is the way she bends her knees,
And this is the way she dances."

The leader holds out both hands to the others, then recites the verse, showing the way the fingers must move. The others are to follow the leader's finger movements with their own fingers.

1. Make both hand into fists. 2. The leader then says, "This is the way the teacher stands," and raises the first fingers of both hands. 3. The leader goes on to say, "This is the way she holds her hands," and raises all the fingers on both hands. 4. Then the leader says, "This is the way she bends her knees," and keeping all the fingers up, only bends

the second fingers of both hands. 5. The leader says, "And this is the way she dances." With the second fingers still bent down and with all the fingers and thumbs still up, only the third fingers of both hands must be moved up and down, using a dancing-like movement.

The leader must watch to see the others make no mistakes. Whoever makes a mistake is 'out'. The last one 'in' becomes the new leader.

* * *

The 'Neivie-nick-nack' guessing game. (With closed fists.)

Neivie, neivie, nick-nack,
Which han' will ye tak?
Tak the richt, tak the wrang,
I'll beguile ye if I can.

*　　　*　　　*

Mrs Dunlop had a wee shop
And all she sold was candy rock
Candy rock, a penny a stick
Take a lick and let wan drop.

*　　　*　　　*

Eettle, ottle, black bottle
Eettle, ottle, oot
If you want a piece on jam
Just call oot!

Eerie oarie roon the table
Eerie oarie oot
If ye're able, eat the table
You – are – out!

"What did the big chimney say to the wee chimney?
 "You're o'er young to smoke."

*   *   *

"What do you get when you cross a sheepdog with a jelly?"
 "The collie-wobbles."

*   *   *

And then there were the Englishman, Irishman and Scotsman jokes ... with the Scot always coming off best, of course!

The Englishman went into a room and saw a pound note on a table. He was just about to put it into his pocket when he heard a voice saying: "I'm the ghost of Auntie Mabel, that pound note must stay on the table."

Then the Irishman went into the room and saw the pound note on the table. Just as he was stretching out his hand to put it in his pocket he heard a voice saying: "I'm the ghost of Auntie Mabel, that pound note must stay on the table."

So the Scotsman went in and immediately stuck the money in his pocket and said: "I'm the ghost of Davy Crockett, this pound note must stay in my pocket!"

*   *   *

Ali bali, ali bali who's got the ball?
I've not got it, in my pocket
Ali bali? ali bali who's got the ball?

*   *   *

Where was Hitler when the lights went out?
Up Sauchiehall Street smokin' a dout;
The dout was wee and so was he,
Where was Hitler when the lights went out?

*   *   *

Salvation Army free from sin
Went tae heaven in a corned beef tin
The corned beef began tae smell
The Salvation Army went tae hell!

*   *   *

Marty Farty
Had a party
All the farts were there.
Tooty Fruity
Did a beauty
So they went to Ayr.

*   *   *

"Do you know the rope joke?"
"No."
"Aw, skip it!"

*   *   *

A wee boy needed to go to the toilet (so this playground joke goes), and he asked out of the class. The teacher said he would let him provided he said his alphabet first. The wee boy recited, "A B C D E F G H I J K L M N O Q R S T U V W X Y X."

The teacher asked, "Where's the 'P'?"
"Half-way doon ma leg!"

*   *   *

Three polar bears were sitting on an iceberg. The father bear said, "I've a tale to tell."

The mummy bear said, "I've a tale to tell too."
And the wee baby bear said, "My tale is told."

*   *   *

One, two, three, four
Mary at the cottage door
Eating cherries off a plate
Five, six, seven, eight.

*   *   *

One potato, two potato
Three potato, four
Five potato, six potato
Seven potato ... more!

    *   *   *

Willie cut his fether's throat,
Stained wi' blood his Sunday coat.
His mither cried in tones impassioned,
"Stupid ass! yer claes are rationed!"

    *   *   *

Said the wee red rooster to the wee red hen,
'You haven't laid an egg since I don't know when.'
Said the wee red hen to the wee red rooster,
'Ye don't come roon as often as ye use'ter!'

    *   *   *

Homework, moanwork
Cross it oot an' groanwork
Homework, neatwork
Drive ye aff yer heidwork!

    *   *   *

Eeny meeny miny mo
Sit the baby on the po
When he's done wipe his bum
Throw the paper up the lum.

Things I Remember
My Teacher Said

"If I have failed to teach you then you must do it yourself. Read the *Glasgow Herald* or the *Scotsman* each day, and you will educate yourself through life."

"We Scots are a fortunate race. When the Angles landed in Northumbria, the acute Angles went north; the obtuse ones went south."

Whenever there was some uncertainty in school-life, he would say, "Sic a Shirra-muir!"
(Such a Sherrifmuir, meaning a confused situation with both sides claiming victory.)

"Never sell yer hens on
a wet day in Paisley!"
(We believed it to
mean you should be
wise and thrifty.)

"This is your school. You don't learn to swim in a field."

"Sit down! I might as well be talking to that gas-bracket."

"Remember. Ignorance dies more slowly than knowledge grows."

"Tak yer greasy heids aff yer desks an' sit up. Otherwise I'll tak ye doon tae the slacher-house an' gi'e ye a dustin."

"If you don't believe me at least believe in yourself."

"You've every kind of sense except common sense!"

"Believe me, boy, you cannae lead the band unless you understand the music."

"All today's sums are B.I.W." She then proceeded to write the sums on the blackboard with the dreaded abbreviation underneath. (Belt If Wrong)

Never pretend to know when you don't."

...but I can't say it ever did me any harm.

From the P.E. teacher. "I think you lot learned to dance on a train with no toilets!"

"In this life we're all just riding the bike of inexperience."

"What you think you are, you are."

"Everyone has a talent. Whether they believe it or not."

"Each sentence writes the character of the author ... and there are some characters in this class!"

"Many of your books are not as dull as their readers!"

"In life never think that price and value mean the same thing."

"Forget Confucius and read Cicero. He said, 'We are in bondage to the law in order that we may be free'."

*   *   *

2. The Wee Rascals!

A teacher of an infant's class in Dunfermline, was informing her class of her rules for asking out to use the toilet.

"Remember, put your hand up if you wish to go to the toilet. If it's to pass water, tell me it's a number one. If it's to pass a solid, tell me it's a number two.

Not long after this instruction a wee boy put up his hand. "Sorry miss, but what's the number for a fart?"

*　　　*　　　*

The teacher at a Stirling school was off with a broken leg. However due to a temporary shortage of staff, she hobbled in each day to help in the school office.

"How's your teacher, now?" asked one parent of her offspring.

"Well, she's back at school, but she still cannae teach."

*　　　*　　　*

"Are you sure you did your reading last night, Agnes?" queried the teacher in a Gourock school.

"I did, miss. I read it to my father."

"And what did he say?"

"He was sleeping at the time, Miss."

*   *   *

The school inspector was intercepted in the playground of an Edinburgh School by an eleven year old boy.

"You the inspector, mister?"

"Yes, I am."

"Well, are we glad to see you," said the boy with a mischievous glint and a knowing wink. "This is the first day yon Headie's been at school for months."

*   *   *

A wee boy in a Glasgow school was spotted by his teacher putting a pound note into his pocket.

"Is that your money? demanded the teacher.

"A' fun it," came the determined reply.

"Are you sure it was lost?" queried the teacher.

"Sure. A' saw the wumman lookin fur it, miss."

*   *   *

In the corridor of a Glasgow school there was a fish tank, and also a smaller tank with frog-spawn. One day a child noticed that a frog had appeared. The children and a passing teacher gathered around the tank. Just as the teacher was opening her mouth to tell the class about this development, a voice was heard. "Gae it a kiss, miss, and ye might get yersel' a man."

* * *

"Paul! Did you or did you not push Margaret to the ground in the playground today?" demanded a teacher in an Edinburgh school.

"Well, sir, it wasn't me. Anyway, Brian did it with me."

* * *

Susan, a small pupil in a Glasgow school was forever fidgeting, and on inspection by her teacher, found to be fiddling with an old safety pin. The pin was duly confiscated.

Sometime later, the teacher had occasion to call Susan out to her desk. This caused merriment among the class.

"What are you all laughing at?" asked the teacher.

"Please, miss," ventured one boy, "the pin wis haudin' up her knickers."

*　　　*　　　*

"You never do your homework properly, Weir," came the exasperated voice of an Oban teacher. "Why do you play football, morning, noon and night, Weir?"

"Just for kicks, sir."

"Come out here and hold out your hand!"

*　　　*　　　*

The six year old in Glasgow was told to stand in the queue for free dinners. She immediately burst out crying.

"What's the matter," demanded the dinner lady.

"I couldnae eat three dinners."

*　　　*　　　*

"Please miss, we've oot oor single-end and into a new hoose," confided one wee Glasgow pupil.

"That nice, McGhee. And do you have your own room?"

"Aye, and so's ma big sister, and we don't have to sleep in a recess bed any longer ... but ma faither still has tae sleep wi' ma mammy."

*　　　*　　　*

"When you leave secondary school, I hope that most of you will go on to further education; either university, college or night school," said the teacher at a Paisley school, hoping to encourage her pupils to greater educational heights.

One wee girl's response indicated that, perhaps, she was not suitable material for her teacher's ambitions.

"Sure ye need a torch tae go tae night school, miss."

*   *   *

Wee Fiona would never admit to making a mistake.

"What happened to the question mark at the end of this sentence?" asked her teacher at a Perth school.

"I just left it in my pencil, miss."

*   *   *

Charlie was the dunce of his class in Govan. Most days he was relegated to the front seat.

One day, as he sat twirling his thumbs, just looking vacantly into space, Old Tam, his teacher, became aware of the twirling, and stopped what he was doing to look at Charlie. All noise in the class ceased as pupils and teacher, stared at the twirling thumbs.

"Is that the only thing you can do?" shouted Old Tam.

"Oh, naw, sir," came the reply. "I can dae this."

And he changed his twirling thumbs – to anti-clockwise.

Everybody, including Old Tam, burst into fits of laughter.

The offspring of a particularly dysfunctional family in Paisley, was given a bawling out by the teacher, and told he would not be allowed out at the interval.

"Do a' no' get ony time aff for good behaviour?" he enquired.

The infant teacher was harassed. The primary three class had all gone to the toilets after a gym lesson. A great deal of noise could be heard, especially from the boys' cubicles.

"I'm going to come in there and smack the next bottom that makes a noise."

* * *

"Tell me something bad about the witches in Macbeth, Smith," asked the English teacher in an Aberdeen school.

"They couldnae spell, sir."

"Smith, yer patter's like watter!"

"Aye – an your words are absurd!"

* * *

A wee boy in an Aberdeen school, who was normally well behaved, seemed to be always in trouble in class during winter. Part of the punishment was being made to sit beside the wall, near the teacher.

"I think your behaviour changes when the weather gets cold, Blair," chided the teacher.

"Aye, I like sitting next to the radiator, miss," he confided.

* * *

The history teacher in a Paisley school was in full flight. "When I was your age," he proudly told the class, "I could recite all the Scottish battles, and in their correct order."

A voice from the back loudly announced. "Aye, but only wan or two had been fought back then."

*   *   *

Wee Tommy went up to the teacher's desk in a Glasgow school, and proudly handed over a lovely bunch of flowers.

"Are these for me?" she trilled. "You must have a lovely garden."

"Naw – A just jouked through the cemetery this morning."

*   *   *

"Where were the ancient Kings of Scotland crowned, McWilliams?" asked the teacher of a Dundee School.

"At Scone, sir."

"Why Scone, MacWilliams?"

"So they could have them wi' their tea, sir!"

*   *   *

"In this class, I'm God!" thundered the frustrated Edinburgh teacher.

From the back of the class came a voice. "Well, see if you can stop the rain for the interval!"

*   *   *

To stop pupils in an Ayrshire class all shouting out the answers at once, the teacher pronounced that when he asked a question, the pupils should put up their hands if they knew the answer.

There was silence and then one wee lad's hand shot up.

"Yes, Miller?" asked the teacher.

"Just testin', sir!" came the cheeky reply.

* * *

Five year old James, in Kilmarnock, who had been most apprehensive of going to school in the first place, arrived home after his first day.

"Well, ma wee-man," greeted his dad. "How was it?"

"Great, dad! I enjoyed it."

"It'll probably be even better tomorrow."

"What! Have I got to go back ... again?"

* * *

A frustrated teacher was giving out the results of a class test.

"Jamieson, have you no grey matter in that head of yours? It seems to me it is full of nothing but Mickey Mouse."

"Disnae matter to me, miss."

* * *

"You were caught urinating in the school swimming pool, Montford. What have you to say for yourself?" asked the Edinburgh master.

"But, sir. Everybody pees in the pool."

"That may be so, but not off the side!"

The History teacher in an Oban school was clearly in a creative mood. "What do you think, Crighton, that Robert the Bruce would have said to his mother before he left for the Battle of Bannockburn?"

"Cheerio, mammy!"

*　　　*　　　*

The history teacher at an Edinburgh school, was in full flight about the new Scottish Parliament.

"Brenda, as a proud Scot, what is your mother-tongue?"

"Pink, sir."

Role playing, public speaking and gaining confidence, was what a Renfrew teacher was trying to instil, in some small measure, in her charges. "Right, Andrew. I want you to be like your father. Now, address the class."

"Onybody fancy goin' doon tae the rub-a-dub-dub, fur a wee hauf an' a hauf pint?"

*   *   *

"Going by this composition on economics, Stewart, you must think money grows on trees in Glasgow!"

"Naw, miss. Oot the holes-in-the-wa's."

*   *   *

It had been snowing in Stirling, and the school had closed at lunch-time. A thaw had followed and the children were all back at school. The first period was R.E.

"And what did you ask God for in your prayers last night, Anthony?"

"Mair snow, miss."

*   *   *

At an Ardrossan school, a pupil was overheard by his teacher using a *very* bad word.

"Easton!" she shouted. "You mustn't use that word. Where did you get it?"

"Ma daddy says it, miss."

"Well, that doesn't matter. You don't even know what it means."

"I do. It means Rangers have lost!"

*　　　*　　　*

The wee Aberdonian girl met her mother at the school gate after her first day at school.

"How did it go, Mary?"

"Fine, apart fae a wifie, cryed teacher, wha keeps spilin' the fun."

*　　　*　　　*

The wee rascal at a Forfar school arrived back in the classroom after the interval, sporting a cut under an eyebrow.

The teacher took one look at him and exclaimed. "You're going to get a black eye."

"But, sir," wailed the pupil. "I thought you were only allowed to give me the strap!"

*　　　*　　　*

The teacher in a Perthshire school set her class some mental arithmetic.

"If there were a hundred sheep in a field, and seventeen escaped through a hole in the fence, how many would be left in the field?"

A hand went up right away. "Nane, miss."

"No, Craig, it's eighty-three."

"It cannae be, miss. If seventeen got oot the hole, the rest o' the flock wid just follow."

*   *   *

"Thanks for the Tunnock's chocolate biscuits you gave me yesterday, Beryl. I shared them out with the other teachers in the staff room. I did notice they were somewhat melted. Did you have them near the radiator?"

"No, miss. Ma mammy hides them in her knickers when she takes them oot the factory."

*   *   *

At the end of the R.E. lesson, the teacher at a Glasgow school decided to test her class's knowledge on the bit of the Bible they had just read.

"OK – who was Peter?"

"Please miss, he's a rabbit."

*   *   *

The teacher was red-faced in exasperation at his class.

"I will not begin until this room settles down!" He boomed.

A voice from the rear of the class echoed. "Well ye shouldna have been oot on the booze last night."

3. In the Classroom

The wee boy in a Falkirk school stood at the teacher's desk, and asked if she had anything to cure hiccups? She immediately gave his face a slap. "I bet that's cured your hiccups, MacAuslin," she said.

"No, miss," he wailed. "It's fur Gerry in the second row."

*   *   *

The teacher at an Edinburgh school, told her class of five year olds that the following year they would become Primary Two. "Then you'll have to stay in school until three o'clock, you can have school dinners if your parents wish, and you will go on to book two for reading."

A wee girl put up her hand. "Please, miss, will my name still be Margaret?"

*   *   *

The new domestic science teacher in a Glasgow school was keen to experiment with creative ideas. One day she put small pieces of a variety of meats on plates, and asked the pupils to guess their origin.

With one particular meat she gave the class a

clue. "They roam about in the Highlands, and it's also a name your mummy sometimes calls your daddy."

"Well, I'm certainly no' eatin' that!" exclaimed one small girl.

*   *   *

"Sleep is essential. Everyone should get at least eight hours every night," the Edinburgh teacher told her class. "Some people sleep lightly, some very soundly. Some people snore." She concluded.

Wee Susan, the class extrovert, had her hand up immediately.

"Sure, miss, snoring is farting at night."

*   *   *

The eight year old in an Edinburgh school was allocated an older type of desk. A remnant of a byegone age, it had a hole where the inkwell had once sat.

"Is that the bit the wires from the PC go through, miss?"

*   *   *

The major issues with Miss Armstrong were always, 'the environment' and the need for 'integrity throughout life'. She emphasised both whenever the opportunity arose.

One day she asked the class. "If you saw someone drop a five pound note on the pavement what would you do?"

The answer from one zealous wee girl was quick. "Please, miss, pick it up and put it in a litter bin."

*   *   *

In a Port Glasgow primary school, the teacher announced to the class on their first morning that the Head would be coming into their classroom, to welcome them all to the school.

After the Head had come and gone, one wee astonished girl exclaimed, "He's got arms and legs too!"

*   *   *

A boy entered the classroom of a Clydebank school, and asked the new technical teacher to go and see the headmaster in his study.

The teacher was unsure at leaving the class of boys alone, especially with all the potentially dangerous tools available. However he told them to get on with their work, and that he would be back in a minute.

He was therefore disconcerted, when one boy at a bench at the front informed him. "Sir, you forgot tae pit oor haunds in the vices. Mister MacLaughlan aye does that when he leaves us alane in the classroom."

*   *   *

It was RE and the zealous teacher at an Edinburgh school was reassuring the children on the love of the Almighty.

"God is always with us, children, even though we can't see him," she pronounced solemnly.

One wee boy's hand shot up and he declared his agreement of her statement.

"Sure He's the wan that operates the magic doors at Tesco's, miss."

*   *   *

The English teacher at a very respectable Edinburgh school, was talking about famous Scots throughout the ages.

"If you could spend a day talking to any one person, dead or alive, who would you chose?"

"The living one, sir."

*   *   *

The subject was, 'The Auld Alliance', and the Edinburgh teacher had gone on to talk about his recent holiday in Paris.

"Right, Jenkins. You tell us. Who was the Hunchback of Notre Dame?"

"I'm not sure, sir."

"Does the name, Quasimodo, not ring a bell, Jenkins?"

*   *   *

Parents were asked to put names on all garments worn to a school near Paisley. One day an exasperated teacher was looking through a pile of unclaimed sweatshirts, checking for names.

A little sarcastically she said, "Oh look, this one belongs to Marks and Spencer."

A small child put up her hand. "I think he's in primary one, miss."

*   *   *

"What size of family do you come from, Joseph?" asked the teacher of a primary class in East Kilbride.

"I've got two brothers and three sisters alive. But I had a wee sister who died long ago."

"Oh, I'm sorry to hear your sister died."

"Yes, miss. She died in fancy."

*   *   *

The Kilmacolm primary two teacher, solemnly informed her pupils that they were in this world to help 'lesser mortals'.

The wee boy's hand went up. "Are the children in primary one the 'lesser mortals?"

*   *   *

The teacher in an East Kilbride school always liked to address subjects which were topical. As the film, *Jurrasic Park*, was all the rage, she opted to discuss prehistoric monsters.

"Of course," she observed, "dinosaurs are now extinct."

One small girl immediately queried. "Were you very sad when it happened, miss?"

*   *   *

The primary one class in Edinburgh had started on a Wednesday, and it was now Friday.

"On Monday, children, I will be issuing you with your first reading book."

One wee boy put up his hand. "In that case, miss, I think I'll just go back to nursery school on Monday."

*   *   *

It was a lesson on reproduction in a Highland School. The teacher explained that Mummy and Daddy needed to have sexual relations to produce a baby.

"Any questions?" asked the apprehensive teacher.

A wee girl put up her hand. "Are they uncles or aunts?"

*   *   *

The little girl at the front table in the Cumbernauld class was inconsolable. She cried, sobbed continuously, and would not respond to anything or anyone. Eventually her older brother from another class was brought into see if he could help.

He managed to calm her down, and then informed the child's teacher what the problem was.

"Ma mammy forgot tae gie her a wee hug and kiss at the school gate this morning."

*   *   *

"Do you have any brothers or sisters still to come to school, Peter?" asked a frustrated teacher in a Port Glasgow school.

"No. I'm the youngest, miss."

"Thank God !" came the relieved mutter.

*   *   *

The primary two child was in tears in a Paisley school. When asked by teacher what was wrong, he said his chickens had disappeared. He had drawn two chickens in a cage – and when he coloured-in the cage all black – the chickens disappeared!

*   *   *

Asked to write a sentence with the word, 'windy', in it, one wee chap in Paisley wrote in his jotter.

'My mother hings out the windy to talk to Mrs Lewis next door.'

*   *   *

The geography lesson was in full swing in an Inverness school.

"North is ahead of you, east is on your right, west is on your left. Now, what's behind you, Barclay?"

"The wa', miss."

*   *   *

The Edinburgh teacher announced to the class, that Keith O'Donnell had fallen off his bicycle on the way home from school the previous day, and broken his leg.

After a moment's silence a wee boy put up his hand. "Please, miss, is his bike O.K?"

*   *   *

"Are you all right, Burns ?" asked a concerned Glasgow teacher. "You look ill to me."

"I'm just a wee bit, peelie-wallie today, miss," pronounced the pupil.

"Now, Burns. Just stop and think. Would an English person understand what you've just said?"

"Oh, sorry, miss. I'm just a little, peelie-wallie today."

*   *   *

"Ma mither's got a new fur coat, miss," announced a proud girl pupil to her teacher in a Glasgow school.

"Is it stole?" enquired the teacher.

"Naw! She's paying it up," came the unexpected reply.

*   *   *

The teacher, somewhat tongue-in-cheek, asked little Homer, not exactly the brightest child in the class, if he was called after the Greek poet?

"Naw. Ma faither used tae keep doos."

*   *   *

"What do Robert the Bruce, William the Conqueror and Peter the Great have in common?" asked an Aberdeen teacher.

Up went the hand of the class toe-rag. "Please sir, they all have the same middle name."

*　　*　　*

At a primary school in Perth, the five year old opened a matchbox and proudly displayed the spider within.

Trying to control her desire to scream, the teacher said.

"Patrick, why don't you leave the spider outside at the interval ... its mummy will be sad at being separated from it."

After the interval, Patrick once more

approached his teacher. "Look, miss. I found its mummy too."

*   *   *

The boy, a right dunderheid, was whistling in the Paisley classroom.

"Boy!" shouted the teacher. "You don't go up in this world if you have a bird brain."

"Then why don't you give up teaching, sir, and work a lift ?"

*   *   *

The school inspector was due to sit in with a class at an Edinburgh school, and listen as they participated in a history project.

The teacher informed the class it was essential to impress the inspector. Every time she asked a question, she wanted everyone to put up their hands, regardless of whether or not they knew the answer. However, those who knew the answer should put up their right hand, and those who didn't, their left.

The following day the inspector was indeed most impressed!

*   *   *

The primary class were being instructed in toileting drill at a Perth school. The instructor was the assistant head.

The girls listened as her voice floated over from the boy's cubicles. "Boys, you pull it out its full length and give it a good shake." All the girls burst into hysterical laughter.

Then the assistant head appeared in the girl's toilets. "Now it's your turn, girls. When you use a toilet roll, pull it out its full length, then give it a good shake."

*   *   *

"What was that noise?" demanded a Dundee teacher of a pupil.

"Please, sir, I ... eh ... pumped."

"Don't be silly, boy. Bikes don't fart."

*　　　*　　　*

The domestic science class was in progress. A bundle of materials lay on a table. The harassed teacher pointed to the table and requested. "Rosemary. Find a net curtain."

"Which class is she in, miss?"

*　　　*　　　*

"Please, miss, I saw hundreds of lions at Edinburgh Zoo on Saturday."

"Brian, how many millions of times have I told you not to exaggerate?"

*　　　*　　　*

A teacher at a Glasgow school was welcoming a new arrival to the school.

"And where do you come from, Julie?"

"Partick, miss."

"Which part?"

"All of me, miss."

*　　　*　　　*

"It's ma mither's birthday today, miss. She's twenty-four," confided the small pupil.

"My, she is getting old," wryly observed the Stirling teacher, a tinkle in her eye.

"Ah know. But do you ken she can still ride a bike."

*   *   *

It was a Glasgow school in the east end of the City.

"Patrick. If your mummy went to the Barrows and bought twenty apples for a pound, what would each one be?"

"At that price, rotten, miss."

*   *   *

A maths teacher in Perth used the same expression daily, much to the amusement of her many pupils over the years.

"Look at the board while I run through it."

*   *   *

The teacher was talking about Queen Victoria's interest in Scottish affairs, and how the Queen had lived at Balmoral for a number of years. She was interrupted by a child.

"Sure, miss, she sat on a thorn for over sixty years."

64

*   *   *

The children were back in their class
after gym in the drill hall.

"Miss, ma feet feel funny," exclaimed
one small child.

"You silly child. You've got your
shoes on the wrong feet."

"But miss, these are the only feet
I've got!"

*   *   *

The newly qualified 22-year-old teacher in a
Renfrew school, had been warned that a small seven
year old girl in her new class, was particularly
disruptive.

During the morning the teacher had occasion to
chide the girl for being naughty. The response was
unexpected.

"Ah hate a' yous auld folk!"

*   *   *

The teacher in a Houston school was getting
exasperated.

"Fraser, I asked you if you would like to read
this story?"

"No."

"Fraser, I really meant you *are going* to read this
story. I was just being polite. It's nice to be polite.

So, Fraser, would you like to read this story?"
"No, thank you."

* * *

"Miss, oor wee budgie, Billy, has died."
"Oh, I'm sorry to hear that, Fiona. How long had your family had Billy?"
"We had Billy for nearly seven years, miss."
"And what did Billy die from, Fiona?"
"The vet said it was a fallen womb, miss."

* * *

The wee boy in primary one of an Ayrshire class, suddenly ran from the room. The teacher told the class to fold their arms and behave while she looked for the runaway.

She heard a noise coming from the boys' toilets. Entering she saw that one of the cubicle doors was shut. She knocked.

"Is that you, Roderick?"

Roderick's voice from within was loud and clear.

"No. It's somebody else."

* * *

The teacher in a Glasgow school was talking about the Saints.

"Now, children. Why do you think I'm not called Saint Catherine?"

"Because she was good and she's deid!"

*   *   *

The basic French class for remedial boys was in session. They were learning to count in French. A hand shot up.

"Please, sur, ma faither has French burds." If the teacher thought he was just about to hear a tasty tale of scandal, he was to be disappointed.

"Douze, sir."

*   *   *

4. Parents

One morning a wee Dunfermline boy was walking very slowly to school with his mum.

"Hurry up, Harry, you're going to be late."

"It's O.K. mum, they're open 'till three."

* * *

The teacher in a Glasgow school was reading out the results of a mid-term examination. "Susan, pass. William, pass. Sally, pass. Jimmy, fail."

"Aw, naw," lamented Jimmy. "Noo ma mammy won't let me get a stud in ma nose."

* * *

Does you teacher look old or young, Susan?" asked a child's mother in Helensburgh. After considerable thought the answer came back.

"I suppose it depends whether you sit at the back or the front of the class."

* * *

Notice sent to parents from a Port Glasgow secondary school.

'Your child has been selected for cooking. Parents are expected to contribute twenty pence towards the cost."

*   *   *

Nine-year old Jason came home and informed his Stirling parents that there was to be a 'wee parent-teachers association meeting' at school, the following morning at ten o'clock.

"And just what do you mean by, 'a wee parent-teachers association meeting'? asked his father.

"Well … it's just you two, me, and Miss Harcus the Headteacher."

*   *   *

"We had a visitor to the school today. He is called Charlie Chaplain," said one wee boy to his mother in Edinburgh. It transpired that the school chaplain had visited that day – and his name was indeed Charles!

*   *   *

It was Parents' Night and a sketch had been planned. Twelve children trooped onto the stage, each holding a letter. Unfortunately one wee girl was not in the correct order. What should have read,

Hello Parents, was presented as, *o Hell Parents.*

*   *   *

The single mum was enrolling her child at the school.

"And is there a partner's name?" was the question posed.

"Listen, hen. When ye take hot peas an' vinegar ye don't know which wan made ye fart. Dae ye?"

*   *   *

Absence Notes from Parents

The scribbled note was a torn piece of paper.

'Please excuse Tom

up yours,

Mrs MacDuff

On the other half, which was folded over, it read –

'who was at the doctors for a check–'

'Please excuse, Janice, for being absent yesterday. She was bitten on the buttocks and had to go to the dentist.'

'I held Betty at home yesterday as her mother had a baby. It will not happen again.'

'Please excuse, Graham, if he is not quite himself today. He ate a lot of jelly and cream at a party last night and was a trifle sick.'

Please excuse, James, as he had diarrhoea in his new sandals.'

'Please excuse, Alan, for being absent at present. He has a sore belly as he swallowed a sixpence. I will let you know if there is any change.'

'Please excuse, William, for being absent as he spewed up the whole of the Main Street last night.'

'Please excuse Jenny's absence this week. I have been upside-down with my new carpets being laid.

'Please excuse, Mary, as she has been in bed with her tum.'

'Please do not give James the strap. At home we only use corporal punishment in self-defence.

'Dear Head Waster, …'

*　　　*　　　*

From a P.T.A. newsletter to parents at a certain Glasgow school.

'This is to help you understand what your child's teacher *REALLY* means, when you are discussing progress at Parents' Night.'

TEACHER SPEAK	TRANSLATION
Willie tries ever so hard	Willie's as thick as mince!
Sometimes Willie has difficulty concentrating	Willie's as daft as a brush!
Willie is quite a lively, little chap	Willie's a right wee toe-rag!
Willie has a strong personality	Willie's an awkward wee bugger!
Willie has a great sense of humour	Willie's work would make the cat laugh!
Willie is a neat writer	Willie cannae spell to save himself!
Willie's a most responsible boy	Willie is responsible for most of the disruption in this class!

TEACHER SPEAK	TRANSLATION
Willie is making satisfactory progress	Willie is so boring I can hardly remember what he looks like!
Willie has a vivid imagination	You should hear some of the excuses Willie comes up with!
Willie is an easy-going child	Willie is the laziest, wee lump I've ever come across!
Willie is a most helpful pupil	Willie is the biggest creep in this school!
Willie excels at sport	The only thing in Willie's heid is fitba'!
Willie works better in a very, small group	You cannae take your eyes off the wee sod for two minutes!

TEACHER SPEAK	TRANSLATION
Willie is good with his hands	Willie cannae stay away from the lassies!
Willie is a born leader	Willie runs a protection racket, and will end up in Barlinnie!
Willie does not always accept authority easily	I assume Willie's father is still in Barlinnie?
Willie is a rather solitary child	Willie smells something awful.

*   *   *

Young Glen came home from his school in Helensburgh, looking rather pained. "And what's the matter with you today?" enquired his mother.

"We learned to spell, 'October', today."

"So, what's wrong with that ?"

"Well, it's November tomorrow, and I'll need to start again."

*   *   *

The five year old girl in Glasgow, was delivered by her mother to the primary one classroom. An envelope was thrust into the teacher's hand and the mother quickly disappeared.

It read: 'Please excuse Marlyn's language. She takes after her father,'

*   *   *

The Glasgow teacher had a hyper-active child in her class, who at times was most disruptive. Eventually she sent a letter to the mother, inviting her to come into school.

"I know the problem," exclaimed the understanding mother. "You see it's an allergy. Oor doctor says not to give him anything with 'E's' in it. So you see it's difficult when the wee soul cannae even have things like bread and cheese."

*   *   *

The proud mother in Hamilton knit her offspring a nice yellow jumper. The wee boy was duly sent off to school wearing it.

That evening the mother, ever so casually, asked if anyone had mentioned the beautiful new jumper?

"Oh, yes," he replied to his mother's delight. "At the interval the jannie shouted, "Hey, you, canary. Keep away fae they windows wi' that ball!"

*   *   *

The father of a little Edinburgh pupil asked what her new teacher in primary two looked like?
"The same as Miss Carrington – but with a different face."

*   *   *

The red-faced Aberdeenshire farmer came to see the teacher of his son's class at the small, community school.

"What's aw this aboot spellin 'tattie' wi' a 'p' ?"

*   *   *

And it was the same farmer, who at parent's night, when told by the headmaster that, "We will give your children the finest education to match any in Scotland," angrily remonstrated. "Aye, an when they loons are so clever, wha's goin' tae pull ma neeps?"

*   *   *

Wee Jim was delivered by his mother to the classroom door of the East Kilbride school.

"Nice to see you back, Jim, after your bad cold," said the teacher. Just then wee Jim had a coughing fit.

"Well, Jim," observed the teacher," you seem to

be coughing much easier now."

"Yer dead right," came the mother. "He's been up practising aw night."

*   *   *

5. The News Book/ Daily Diary/Poems

(See weans – they'd get you hung!)

Notice stuck on the front door of a school at Parents' Night.

'Please do not believe everything your child tells you about us … and we won't believe everything they write about you in their day book.'

*　　　*　　　*

The teacher in Paisley encouraged the class to write something about any pets they had. They were to start off by stating the pet's name.

One girl's entry started thus:

'My dog's Mental.'
(It proved to be its name – and nature.)

*   *   *

From the day book of a nine year old in Edinburgh.

'My mother is a soprano. She just loves to sin in a choir.'

*   *   *

The small pupil in a Glasgow educational establishment, wrote in his diary.

'I live in a wee house in a big house.'

It transpired his home was a multi-storey flat.

*   *   *

A weel-kent Headteacher in the Inverclyde area is known for her fashionable dress sense, which usually includes colour co-ordinated tights.

She was therefore amused to be shown by one of her teaching staff the day book of a pupil.

'Mrs X is very smartly dressed. She always has matching tits.'

*   *   *

A teacher was mystified by an entry in a day book. It read:

'My daddy shaves his windscreen every day.'

At Parents' Night all was revealed. It transpired he had been scraping ice off the windscreen during a cold spell of weather.

*   *   *

The father of a pupil at a Greenock school, had business in Paris. Despite a heavy cold he went ahead with the trip.

Some months later, he was amused to read in his nine-year-old daughter's school diary …

'Dad flew to France with flu.

Oh, what a thing to do.

And now in French he'll need to say,

Atchoo! Atchoo! Atchoo!'

*   *   *

From a Perth school news book.

'I have a worm called Ian. He lives in a jar of earth. He is very kind.'

*　　　*　　　*

In his news book, a young golf enthusiast in Edinburgh wrote:
'When I grow up I would like to be our club's intercourse champion.'

*　　　*　　　*

Entry from an Edinburgh school daily diary.
'My dad can speak Spanish. He can say Madrid and Benidorm,'

*　　　*　　　*

Entry in the day book at a Perth school.
'Last night Daddy put me to bed as Mummy was out with another man.'
When the mother read this at Parents' Night, she quickly hurried over to the teacher and explained.
"My brother and I partner each other at bridge every Tuesday night."

*　　　*　　　*

Entry in a day book in a primary class in Helensburgh.
'Mummy took us to seven public houses.'
Mummy was quick to point out at Parents' Night, that the family had joined the National Trust for Scotland!

*   *   *

Entry in a daily diary in Glasgow.

'My mummy says that kissing daddy is like drinking tea without milk or sugar.'

*   *   *

From an Aberdeen school news book.

'At my Auntie Audrey's wedding I was sick on the dance floor. She probably won't invite me to the next one.'

*   *   *

From the day book in a school in Paisley.

'My big sister's marriage is over. She is back living with us. The marriage was never consumed.'

*   *   *

Daddy went red when he saw this one.

'Last night about two o'clock I heard a noise and saw a burglar coming in downstairs. I woke Daddy and Mummy. Mummy phoned for the police but Daddy stayed in bed.'

*   *   *

'My Mummy and Daddy will try to get me a wee sister during our holidays in Spain.'

*   *   *

Oh, dark and gloomy, horrible school
Thou bring'st a mem'ry of teachers cruel.
Of you and lessons the teachers rule
Oh, dark and gloomy, horrible school.

Why 'twas invented I do not know,
With prefects' lines written row by row;
Also 'puni-echkies' in ceaseless flow
Why 'twas invented I do not know.

*   *   *

School is very boring
With teachers always roaring
Always bawling in your ear
And you pretending not to hear.

When teachers enter the room,
Every single thing turns gloom,
Teachers fat and teachers thin
Always turn us outside in.

*   *   *

That brutal mass of leather
That causes so much pain,
A horrible contraption;
Who can explain?
It should be melted down
Or even turned to felt;
Anything, anything but
Our teacher's belt.

*   *   *

If I had piles of money
D' y' know what I would buy?
I'd buy a pound of gelignite
And put it in a pie.

I'd sent it to Mrs Richardson
Down at our wee school,
And, when the pie was opened
Wouldn't I just drool?

I'd watch each brick go up in the air,
I'd watch each strap come down,
I'd watch each horrible school book
Go flying o'er the town.

It really is a shame,
It's a pity that I'm broke
It would be nice to see our school,
Go up in a cloud of smoke.

*   *   *

Our playground is shrinking
And so I am thinking
That, if it gets smaller
And we're fatter and taller,
There's going to be jostling,
before they start squeezing
Let's hope I'm leaving!

*   *   *

I started off in primary one,
Reading and writing and having fun
Through primary I graduated
Not knowing the work to which I was fated.

Then came the juniors in primary three;
Away with the overall of which I was free.
Exams then did flow, these I despise
Then won my first and very last prize.

Upstairs I went on to primary five,
There to madness my teacher did drive.
Her patience rewarded by doing my best
And sometimes excelling myself in a test.

Then at last a senior was I
Proud of the fact, my head in the sky.
Suddenly brought down to earth with the strains
Expected of seniors exerting their brains.

Schooldays for me are waning I fear
At this the end of my very last year,
I look back with joy, sometimes a sigh
Yes I'll leave this old school with a tear in my eye.

*   *   *

Unhappy band of pupils
If schoolward you will tread
With Big Jackie as your teacher
And worries – in your head.

They're happy if you labour,
But woeful if you shirk;
You're hungry after lunches,
And after that – more work.

But maybe after reading
This trial, nay this blight
I think, perhaps, you will agree
That teachers are – all right.

*   *   *

(To the tune of *Auld Lang Syne*.)

If all the teachin' were forgot,
And never brought to mind,
We'd live a life of luxury
'T would be heavenly divine.

The day would start at twelve o'clock,
And finish just at four,
We'd do no work, but fool around
Then just walk out the door.

No homework of course, no punishments to do,
No prefects would be there,
No French, maths or grammar to do
We wouldn't have a care.

*　　　*　　　*

Monday morning – moans and groans,
Grammar, science, spelling;
What's the teacher got for us?
Really, there's no telling.

Tuesday morning – "Super day!",
Geography, gym, music.
Then it's English, what a bore!
Enough to make you sick.

Wednesday morning "Not so good",
'rithmetic, history, sewing.
Next, it's writing and poetry
Well, that's not just so boring.

Thursday morning – "Better and better",
Spelling, Bible, gym;
Climbing wallbars, climbing ropes
Enough to keep you slim.

Friday morning – "Weekly Test!!",
Something we all dread,
But then the thought of two days free
Goes floating through my head.

*   *   *

This is a pome what I rite,
The teecher says it is a must,
To show how smart we are and brite,
Always up ther amung the fust.

I know our spelins sometims slip,
Our grammer and countin too,
But even Homer used to trip,
Or was it nod – and so do you.

Our techer teeches us dead good
To reed and rite and paint
And even if our heads is would
We wear our halos like the siants.

We'll be a credit to our clas
Be kind and do no killin,
But if, perchance, we dinna pass.
You must admit, we're willin!

        *   *   *

Seven days to go now,
And we're shakin' in our shoes,
We tremble at the word-
We've got 'Exam time' blues!

The timetables have been put up-
We know the day to dread,
Now we're flickin' through the pages
Of the books we should have read.

We'll study when we are at home,
And study with a zest -
To try and let our parents know
We're going to do our best!

        *   *   *

6. Exams and Clangers

The teacher at an Aberdeen school was a kindly soul, who always managed to say something positive about everyone in her class, regardless of the quality of their work.

One day, during a class test, she was making her way around the desks, meting out praise and encouragement as usual. When she got to wee Jim's desk, she leaned over his work and then pronounced. "That's a nice, new pencil you have, Jim."

*　　　*　　　*

Spelling can be a problem, especially in essays and compositions. In one Glasgow school the subject set was, 'The Royals'.

The following is an extract from one offering.

'The kween and the chookkoenbra sumtyms go to the pallis of hollyrude.'

*   *   *

From an interpretation exercise set in a Paisley school: The passage given was all about ships and docks. The question posed was, 'What is a wharf?'

One answer was, 'A little man who never grows up.'

*   *   *

In answer to a question set in a Dundee school. 'Name a Scottish Institution which gives out loans', the answer was unexpected.

'My father.'

*   *   *

A teacher in East Kilbride, gave her class an arithmetical problem involving two trains leaving Glasgow Central for London. She gave them data on leaving times, average speeds and distance covered. They were to calculate the arrival time.

The answer from one pupil was simply put. 'Phone British Rail at the Central. They are very helpful in such matters.'

*   *   *

Asked in a class test held in a Perthshire school, for the definition of water, wee Peter wrote. 'It is a colourless liquid which turns brown when you put your hand in it.'

*   *   *

From a R.E. class test in a school near Paisley.

Question: 'What do you called the
                    King of Egypt?'
Answer: 'Elvis.'
Question: 'Which is the most important
                    commandment?'
Answer: 'Thou shalt not admit adultery.'

*   *   *

The school inspector came to visit a small, two-classroom school in Invernessshire. The teacher, who taught both small classes, informed the inspector that the younger group were surprisingly adept for their age at mental arithmetic.

Thus encouraged, the inspector asked the class, just to get things going, what 'one and one' was? The entire class looked blank. He tried again with the same result.

Turning to the teacher, he exclaimed, "I thought you told me they were good at mental arithmetic."

"And so they are," defended the teacher. "You just didn't ask the question properly. Here, let me demonstrate."

"Noo, class, whit's yin and yin?"

In unison the class replied, "Twaa!"

*   *   *

The English teacher was in a creative mood at a school in Renfrew.

"I want you to write a composition. I want you to express yourself – let it come from within you."
One pupil's effort included the following:

'Inside I have cornflakes, milk and sugar, half a Bounty bar and a cup of tea. Also soup, chips and a burger.'

*　　　*　　　*

The girls at a Greenock school were asked to write a composition on the subject of 'make-up'.

One effort ran thus : 'My big sister massacres her eyes before she goes out.'

*　　　*　　　*

The teacher at a Paisley school was instructing the class on the use of the dictionary. They were told to search the dictionary for an interesting word around which they should construct a sentence.

One small child wrote, 'My sock is sanctified'.

The puzzled teacher requested an explanation, and the pupil opened his dictionary and produced the definition of sanctified … 'a holy place.'

*　　　*　　　*

The metric system was being introduced into a Glasgow school. Instead of inches, feet and yards,

pupils were taught in centimetres, metres, kilo-
metres, etc.

Asked to demonstrate their understanding of the
new terms in an essay, one class wit wrote. 'My aunt
arrived at the Central station and I was centimetre.'

*　　　*　　　*

The Falkirk teacher asked her class to write a
composition about Christmas. This is part of one
girl's effort.

'Santa lives with God but at Christmas flits to the
Co-operative.'

*　　　*　　　*

"Where do spiders have their home?" was the
question asked by a Port Glasgow teacher.

"In a website, sir"

*　　　*　　　*

From an essay foolishly set by an Edinburgh
teacher. The subject given was, 'My Teacher.'

One sentence, from a particularly gifted pupil's
essay, caught her eye.

'She enters the classroom each day with great
gusto, her elastic stockings flapping in the breeze.'

*　　　*　　　*

The subject was 'plurals' in a Glasgow classroom.

"And what is the plural of potato?" the teacher asked.

"Mashed, miss."

*　　*　　*

An H.M. Inspector arrived in a Clydebank school classroom. The teacher, who had only recently qualified, was nervous.

The inspector selected a name from the register.

"Henderson. Stand up."

A large, red-headed lad got to his feet.

"What's three times nine, Henderson?"

"Twenty-seven, sir."

"What's eleven times eight?"

"Eighty-eight, sir."

"What's six times seven?"

"Forty-two, sir."

"Quite good, Henderson."

"Quite good!" exclaimed the pupil. "Jings, it's bloody perfect."

*　　*　　*

'What is Hogmanay?' was the question set in an interpretation exercise at a Glasgow school.

One of the answers was, 'It is a type of wood used in Scotland at the New Year.'

*　　*　　*

The invigilator at an Edinburgh school, thought she saw a suspicious movement at the far end of the gym-hall being used for the third year exams.

Quickly moving up the passage she discovered a boy, leaning half under the table, whispering into a mobile phone.

"And just what do you think you are doing on the phone in the middle of an examination?" she testily demanded in a loud whisper.

"Please, miss, I was just ... eh ... phoning my father for a lift home."

"Give me that phone!" she replied, whilst at the same time grabbing the instrument from the startled pupil. Hearing a girl's voice coming from the mobile, she held it to her ear.

"Now, the way you tackle question twelve (c) is this ..."

*　　　*　　　*

The inspector to a Glasgow school was well known for his emphasis on maths.

Selecting a class he proceeded to set them problems in logic.

"Children, I am going to give you a sequence of numbers. I want you to tell me the odd one out. 5 – 7 – 10 – 14 – 19 – 25 – 33."

To the teacher's horror, wee Chan, immediately stuck up his hand.

"Thirty-three, sir."

"Well done," said the inspector. Turning to the

teacher he observed. "An impressive class, Miss Thompson," and left the classroom.

The teacher immediately went over to wee Chan and said. "That was wonderful, Chan. How did you work it out?"

"Easy, miss," he replied. "You get fried rice with all the rest."

*   *   *

The question posed by the inspector to a class in an Edinburgh school was, "What part do managers have in industry?"

The answer from one boy was clear. "They are part of the higher Archie, sir."

'Scotland's climate is a temporary one.'

*   *   *

'Fort William is found at the bottom of Loch Ness.'

*   *   *

'All crofters drink sherry.'

*   *   *

'Robert the Bruce won a bottle of Bannockburn.'

*   *   *

'The Queen's husband is King Fillip.'

*   *   *

'The Romans built Hadrian's Wall to keep the English out.'

*   *   *

'People are burned alive at Linn Crematorium.'

*   *   *

7. Extra Curricular Activities

The English teacher was charged
with putting on a Nativity Play.
She decided that the children
could improvise, where necessary.

One of the three wise men took
it to extremes. Kneeling in front
of Joseph, Mary and the Baby, he
announced in a very loud voice.

"He's a lovely wean …
and he's certainly got his
mother's chin!"

*   *   *

The Ayr P.E. teacher was announcing the eleven-
and-under school football team for the forthcoming
game.

"McPherson – you're in goal. Williams – you're
right back. Smith – you're left back. And as for you,
Benson – you're a right drawback !"

*   *   *

Further communication by the same P.E. teacher.

"All the boys playing in the school 'B' team on Saturday morning will be pinned to the notice-board."

*　　　*　　　*

The Edinburgh school's old boy had done well. Although still a relatively young man he was worth millions. He was invited to address fifth and sixth years on, 'The Entrepreneurial Spirit.'

At the end of his speech he asked for questions. The first came from a particularly attractive and mature sixth year girl.

"Are you married?"

*　　　*　　　*

The school doctor of a Paisley educational establishment, examined the small boy.

"How are your eyes, son?"

"I can see fine, sir."

"And how are your ears?"

"Well, it's difficult getting the jumper I got from my granny for my birthday over them."

*　　　*　　　*

The primary six choir was entered in the local, Renfrewshire Musical Festival.

One wee girl informed her mother they would be singing, 'without accomplishment'.

*   *   *

A safety poster outside a Glasgow school read ...
   'Careful! Do not kill our children!'
   Underneath, a pupil had added. 'No – wait until a teacher crosses the road.'

*   *   *

Auld Bill, a bachelor, who had taught History and English at an Edinburgh school for many years, always enjoyed his solitary pipe and coffee in the corner of the staff room.

He was therefore most unhappy when a new member of staff, a middle-aged spinster, Miss Heron, took to joining him at break times. She chatted away about this and that, and although Bill tried everything to get rid of her, including blowing gales of smoke in her direction, nothing seemed to work.

In despair after many weeks, he turned to his boys' class during one History lesson on famous Queens of Britain, and solemnly declared. "You know, boys. It is very difficult to get rid of a woman unless you chop her head off."

One hand immediately shot up. "Please, Sir. Ma big brother says it's easy. When he gets fed up wi' a burd he just starts pickin' his nose."

And so it happened. The following day as Miss Heron talked incessantly on and on, Bill put down his pipe and picked furiously at his nose.

Next day, he was once more left at peace with his pipe and coffee.

*   *   *

It was the last two periods on Friday afternoon, and the new teacher at a Dunbartonshire school was taking a class of boys. It was the bottom class of the year but the zealous teacher was determined they would gain something from his lesson.

He had just started when the headmaster stuck his head through the door and exclaimed. "Surely yer no' givin' this lot work. They're unejicable!" And to the astonishment of the teacher, the heidie opened the large window of the ground floor classroom and all the boys eased their way out.

"There – noo we've got peace."

*   *   *

A teacher in an Aberdeen school had a novel way of dealing with any child complaining of toothache.

"Just sit doon and keep nippin' yer bum. That'll tak yer mind aff the toothache."

Apparently it worked.

*   *   *

In the music class, the question was asked, "Who can play a musical instrument?"

"I play with a fruit in the Salvation Army, Sir."

"You mean the flute."

"No, the tangerine."

"Fool – you mean the tambourine!"

*   *   *

In a Paisley school it was approaching Christmas.

"Right, William. You can be one of the Three Wise Men."

"Does that mean I carry the frankenstein, Miss?"

*   *   *

An eleven-year-old Edinburgh girl, somewhat knowing in the ways of the world, arrived at her first year fancy dress party in a costume which left the headteacher nonplussed.

The girl wore a long skirt with a cushion tucked inside at the front. The notice on her back read.

'I should have danced all night!'

*   *   *

A travelling ballet company visited a Glasgow school, to encourage the weans in the finer things of life.

At the end of the performance, the teacher asked if anyone had a question.

"Please, sir, see they wee wummen knockin' aboot on tiptoe. Can they no' just hire bigger wans?"

*   *   *

Young Morag was sleeping in the sick-bay of a certain educational establishment in Hamilton, deposited there by her teacher, 'Old Stucky', when she had complained of feeling ill.

The pupil eventually awoke. It was dark. Looking at her watch she discovered it was after six o'clock. The school was quiet and all locked up. Fortunately her cries for help were heard by the jannie.

*   *   *

"How did the school football match go on Saturday morning, John?" asked the teacher at a Glasgow school.

"Well, sir, we did aw right in the first half, but they brought on two big prostitutes in the second and scored."

*   *   *

Asked what her biggest error of judgement in teaching was, the teacher of a primary one class in Paisley replied.

"It was on the day the class did painting. Instead of painting a flower or a house, I told them they should paint the person next to them!"

110